THE ENGLISH REVOLUTION 1640

AN ESSAY

BY

CHRISTOPHER HILL

1955

LAWRENCE & WISHART LTD

LONDON

First published 1940
Reprinted 1941
Reprinted 1943
Second Edition 1949
Third Edition 1955

Made and Printed in Great Britain by
Charles Birchall and Sons, Ltd., Liverpool and London

CONTENTS

PREFACE

SOME slight changes have been made for the third edition of this essay, first published in 1940. More substantial revision and expansion would be needed to incorporate the results of recent work on the period, especially that of Maurice Dobb in his *Studies in the Development of Capitalism.* Meanwhile this essay must stand as a first approximation, with all its crudities and oversimplifications. For documentary evidence for some of my generalisations the reader may be referred to *The Good Old Cause*, published by Lawrence and Wishart in 1949.

It may help if I attempt here a definition of two terms which seem to have caused some misunderstanding.

I use the word *feudal* in the Marxist sense, and not in the more restricted sense adopted by most academic historians to describe narrowly military and legal relations. By "feudalism" I mean a form of society in which agriculture is the basis of economy and in which political power is monopolised by a class of landowners. The mass of the population consists of dependent peasants subsisting on the produce of their family holdings. The landowners are maintained by the rent paid by the peasants, which might be in the form of food or labour, as in early days, or (by the sixteenth century) in money. In such a society there is room for small handicraft production, exchange of products, internal and overseas trade; but commerce and industry are subordinated to and plundered by the landowners and their State. *Merchant* capital can develop within feudalism without changing the mode of production; a challenge to the old ruling class and its state comes only with the development of the capitalist mode of production in industry and agriculture.

The word *progressive* as used in this essay does not necessarily imply moral approval. It means simply that the tendency or social group so described contributed to the expansion of the wealth of the community. The "progressive" (i.e. capitalist) farming of the sixteenth and seventeenth centuries led to expropriation of many small peasants; the wealth produced by the new methods came into the hands of a small group of profiteers; the village community was broken up. Nevertheless, more wealth *was* produced: the alternative would have been economic stagnation or retrogression. Eighteenth- and nineteenth-century Spain show what such stagnation would have meant for the political and cultural life of the community. In the long run the creation of new wealth by the rise of capitalism in England opened up the possibility of a more equitable distribution at a new level, just as the horrors of the industrial revolution in the nineteenth century created the economic basis for a transition to socialism. Thus although I am far from absolutely "approving" of any tendency which I label "progressive" in the seventeenth century, the suggestion is that *of the then possible alternatives* it was that tendency (because it developed the national wealth) *without which* the advance to a better society would have been impossible. We do not need to idealise "merrie England" to realise that much was lost by the disruption of the mediæval village; but its relative equality and communal spirit had always been accompanied by grinding poverty for the mass of the population, and were doomed by the sixteenth century anyway. Equality and a communal spirit, combined with a reasonable and rising standard of living, only became attainable after capitalism has performed its historical task of laying the industrial foundation for a socialist society. Hence to-day we can at last see our way to realising the dreams of the Levellers and Diggers in 1649.

CHRISTOPHER HILL.

March, 1955

I.

INTRODUCTION

THE object of this essay is to suggest an interpretation of the events of the seventeenth century different from that which most of us were taught at school. To summarise it briefly, this interpretation is that the English Revolution of 1640-60 was a great social movement like the French Revolution of 1789. The state power protecting an old order that was essentially feudal was violently overthrown, power passed into the hands of a new class, and so the freer development of capitalism was made possible. The Civil War was a class war, in which the despotism of Charles I was defended by the reactionary forces of the established Church and conservative landlords. Parliament beat the King because it could appeal to the enthusiastic support of the trading and industrial classes in town and countryside, to the yeomen and progressive gentry, and to wider masses of the population whenever they were able by free discussion to understand what the struggle was really about. The rest of this essay will try to prove and illustrate these generalisations.

The orthodox attitude to the seventeenth-century revolution is misleading because it does not try to penetrate below the surface, because it takes the actors in the revolution at their face value, and assumes that the best way to find out what people were fighting about is to consider what the leaders *said* they were fighting about. We all know that during the seventeenth century England underwent a profound political revolution. Everyone has heard of Oliver Cromwell and his Roundheads, King Charles and his Cavaliers, and we all know that a King of England had his head cut off. But why did this happen? What was it all about? Has it any significance for us at the present day?

These questions are not usually very satisfactorily answered in the text-books. The bloodshed and violence which accompanied the revolution are slurred over as regrettable incidents, when Englishmen for once descended to the wicked continental practice of fighting one another about politics. But that was only because mistakes were made, opportunities for British compromise were missed: what a good thing, the books imply, that we are so much wiser and more sensible to-day! So they do not ever give us reasons which would seem to us sufficient to justify the devotion and the sacrifices of our ancestors in their struggles.

The most usual explanation of the seventeenth-century revolution is one that was put forward by the leaders of the Parliament of 1640 themselves in their propaganda statements and appeals to the people. It has been repeated with additional detail and adornments by Whig and Liberal historians ever since. This explanation says that the Parliamentary armies were fighting for the liberty of the individual and his rights in law against a tyrannical Government that threw him into prison without trial by jury, taxed him without asking his consent, billeted soldiers in his house, robbed him of his property, and attempted to destroy his cherished Parliamentary institutions. Now all this is true—as far as it goes. The Stuarts did try to stop people meeting and holding political discussions, did cut off the ears of people who criticised the government, did arbitrarily collect taxes which were very unequal in their incidence, did try to shut up Parliament and rule the country by nominated officials. All that is true. And although Parliament in the seventeenth century was even less genuinely representative of ordinary people than it is at the present day, still its victory was important as establishing a certain amount of self-government for the richer classes in society.

But further questions are still unanswered. Why did the King become tyrannical? Why did the landed and commercial classes represented in Parliament have to fight for their liberties? During the sixteenth century, under the Tudor rulers, the grandfathers of the Parliamentarians of 1640 were the monarchy's stoutest supporters. What had happened to change their outlook? Parliament had supported Henry VII and Henry VIII and Elizabeth in their efforts to police the country against the anarchy and brigandage of over-mighty subjects, of feudal potentates with their private armies, and England had been made safe for commercialism. Parliament had also supported Henry VIII and Elizabeth in their victorious struggle against the international Catholic Church: money no longer went from England to Rome, British policy was no longer dictated by the interests of a foreign power. Parliament, finally, encouraged Queen Elizabeth in her resistance to the political ally of the Papacy, the Spanish Empire; and the plunder of the New World was thrown open to Drake, Hawkins and the piratical but Protestant seadogs.

The Tudors, in short, were backed by the politically effective classes because the latter did very well out of Tudor rule. Why did the Stuarts, James I and Charles I, lose this support? It was not just because James, who succeeded Elizabeth in 1603, was a particularly stupid man, a Scot who did not understand England, though many historians have seriously argued thus. But one has only to read what James, Charles and their supporters wrote and said, or examine what they did, to see that so far from being merely stupid, they were either able men trying to impose a vicious policy, or men whose ideas were hopelessly out of date and therefore reactionary. The causes of the civil war must be sought in society, not in individuals.

Another school of historians—which we may call "Tory," as opposed to the Whigs—holds that the royal policy was not tyrannical at all, that Charles I, as he told the Court which sentenced him to death, spoke "not for my own right alone, as I am your King, but for the true liberty of all my subjects." Clarendon, who deserted the Parliament in 1642 and later became Charles II's first minister, developed this theory in several volumes of eloquent prose in his *History of the Great Rebellion*; it is now propagated by a number of historians whose political prejudices, royalist or Catholic sympathies, and bias against liberalism in general, make up for their lack of historical understanding. Their idea is that Charles I and his advisers were really trying to protect ordinary people from economic exploitation by a small class of capitalists on the make; and that the opposition which faced Charles was organised and worked up to serve their own purposes by those business men who identified their interests with the House of Commons in politics and Puritanism in religion.

Now, it is true that the English Revolution of 1640, like the French Revolution of 1789, was a struggle for political, economic and religious power, waged by the middle class, the bourgeoisie, which grew in wealth and strength as capitalism developed. But it is not true that as against them the royal Government stood for the interests of the common people: on the contrary, the popular parties proved to be the King's most militant opponents, far more vigorous and ruthless and thorough-going than the bourgeoisie itself.

The interests for which Charles's monarchy stood were not those of the common people at all. It represented the land-owning nobles, and its policy was influenced by a Court clique of aristocratic commercial racketeers and their hangers-on, sucking the life-blood from the whole people by methods of economic exploitation which we shall be considering later on. The middle-class struggle to shake off the control of this group was not merely selfish; it fulfilled a progressive historical function. The sharper-witted landowners were grafting themselves as parasites on to the new growth of capitalism, since their own mode of economic existence no longer sufficed to maintain them. It was necessary for the further development of capitalism that this choking parasitism should be ended by the overthrow of the feudal state. It was to the advantage of the masses of the population that capitalism should be allowed to develop freely. Under the old order, in the century before 1640, real wages for labourers in industry and agriculture fell by more than one half: in the century after 1640 they more than doubled.

The new economic developments of the sixteenth and seventeenth centuries made the old economic and social and political system hopelessly out of date. Those of its defenders who looked regretfully back to the stability and relative security of the peasantry in the Middle Ages were quite unrealistic and in effect reactionary. Their role was the same as that of many liberals at the present day who think how nice it would be if capitalism could still work in the " liberal " nineteenth-century way, without having to resort quite so frequently to fascism and war. But fine words alter no historic processes. History has passed on and left these apologists of an imaginary system standing, just as it left Charles I's defenders.

These two theories, then, are both one-sided. The Whigs stress the progressive nature of the revolution, and slur over the fact that the class that took the lead in the revolution and most profited by its achievements was the bourgeoisie. Their interpretation perpetuates the legend that the interests of the bourgeoisie are identical with those of the nation, a legend obviously convenient for our own day, though so much less true now than in the seventeenth century. The Tories, on the other hand, stress the class nature of the revolution in an attempt to deny its progressiveness and value in its own time, to whitewash feudalism, and to suggest that revolutions never benefit more than a narrow clique. A recent version suggests that all politics is a dirty game, all principles are eye-wash, all revolutions useless.

A third and more familiar theory is emphasised by both sides: that the conflict was to decide which of two religions, Puritanism or Anglicanism, was to be dominant in England. Here, again, the effect of this explanation is to make us pity and misunderstand the men of the seventeenth century, and congratulate ourselves on being so much more sensible to-day: however much Anglicans and Nonconformists may dislike one another personally, we say, they no longer fight in the village street. But this is to miss the point. Certainly religious squabbles fill many pages of the pamphlet literature of the seventeenth century: both sides justified their attitude ultimately in religious terms, believed they were fighting God's battles. But "religion" covered something much wider than it does to-day. The Church throughout the Middle Ages, and down to the seventeenth century, was something very different from what we call a Church to-day. It guided all the movements of men from baptism to the burial service, and was the gateway to that life to come in which all men fervently believed. The Church educated children; in the village parishes—where the mass of the people was illiterate—the parson's sermon was the main source of information on current events and problems, of guidance on economic conduct. The parish itself was an important unit of local government, collecting and doling out such pittances as the poor received. The Church controlled men's feelings and told them what to believe, provided them with entertainment and shows. It took the place of news and propaganda services now covered by many different and more efficient institutions—the Press, the B.B.C., the cinema, the club, and so forth. That is why men took notes at sermons; it is also why the government often told preachers exactly what to preach.

For example, Queen Elizabeth "tuned her pulpits" ("as governing persons now strive to tune their morning newspapers," said Carlyle); she circulated an official book of homilies to all preachers to make sure they said the right things. It was " to be read in every parish church agreeably," and concludes with a sermon in six parts condemning "disobedience and wilful rebellion." Bishops and priests were far more like civil servants, part of the government's administrative machine, than they are at present; and the first to recognise this fact were the ecclesiastics themselves. Bancroft, a prelate of late Elizabethan times, mocked at the Puritan claim to be dealing simply with Church matters. "How far these words Church causes . . . extend!" he cried. "You see into what an infinite sea of affairs they would thrust their elderships."[1] "Presume not," warned the Anglican Hooker, "ye that are sheep, to make yourselves guides of them that should guide you . . . For God is not a God of sedition and confusion, but of order and of peace."[2]

The Church, then, defended the existing order, and it was important for the Government to maintain its control over this publicity and propaganda agency. For the same reason, those who wanted to overthrow the feudal state had to attack and seize control of the Church. That is why political theories tended to get wrapped up in religious language. It was not that our seventeenth-century forefathers were much more conscientious and saintly men than we are. Whatever may be

[1] Bancroft, *A Survey of the Pretended Holy Discipline*, ed. 1593, pp. 281-2.
[2] Hooker, *Of the Laws of Ecclesiastical Polity*, Everyman Edition, I, pp. 95-6.

true of Ireland or Spain, we in England to-day can see our problems in secular terms just because our ancestors put an end to the use of the Church as an exclusive and persecuting instrument of political power. We can be sceptical and tolerant in religious matters, not because we are wiser and better, but because Cromwell, stabling in cathedrals the horses of the most disciplined and most democratic cavalry the world had yet seen, won a victory which for ever stopped men being flogged and branded for having unorthodox views about the Communion service. As long as the power of the State was weak and uncentralised, the Church with its parson in every parish, the parson with honoured access to every household, could tell people what to believe and how to behave; and behind the threats and censures of the Church were all the terrors of hell fire. Under these circumstances social conflicts inevitably became religious conflicts.

But the fact that men spoke and wrote in religious language should not prevent us realising that there is a social content behind what are apparently purely theological ideas. Each class created and sought to impose the religious outlook best suited to its own needs and interests. But the real clash is between these class interests: behind the parson stood the squire.

It is not then denied that the "Puritan Revolution" was a religious as well as a political struggle; but it was more than that. What men were fighting about was the whole nature and future development of English society. This will be illustrated in the following pages, but it is worth showing now that contemporaries knew perfectly well what it was all about, far better, in fact, than many later historians.

It was not merely that, when the victory of the bourgeoisie had been achieved, thinkers like Winstanley, Harrington, Neville, Defoe recognised that the war had been primarily a struggle over property. Shrewd politicians showed in the heat of the contest that they knew well enough who their opponents were. As early as 1603, James I told Parliament that the Puritans—

> "do not so far differ from us in point of religion as in their confused form of policy and parity, being ever discontented

with the present government and impatient to suffer any superiority, which maketh their sects insufferable in any well-governed commonwealth."[1]

The political theorist, Hobbes, describes how the Presbyterian merchant class of the city of London was the first centre of sedition, trying to build a state governed like the republics of Holland and Venice, by merchants for their own interests. (The comparison with the bourgeois republics is constantly recurring in Parliamentarian writings.) Mrs. Hutchinson, the wife of one of Cromwell's colonels, said all were described as Puritans who "crossed the views of the needy courtiers, the proud encroaching priests, the thievish projectors, the lewd nobility and gentry . . . whoever could endure a sermon, modest habit or conversation, or anything good."[2] Baxter, a leading Puritan divine, was even more explicit:

> "A very great part of the knights and gentlemen of England . . . adhered to the King . . . And most of the tenants of these gentlemen, and also most of the poorest of the people, whom the others call the rabble, did follow the gentry and were for the King. On the Parliament's side were (besides themselves) the smaller part (as some thought) of the gentry in most of the counties, and the greatest part of the tradesmen and freeholders and the middle sort of men, especially in those corporations and counties which depend on clothing and such manufactures."[3]

He concluded—

> "Freeholders and tradesmen are the strength of religion and civility in the land; and gentlemen and beggars and servile tenants are the strength of iniquity."[4]

Why he lumped together precisely these classes will shortly become evident.

[1] *Parliamentary History of England*, I, p 982.
[2] *Memoirs of Colonel Hutchinson*, Everyman Edition, pp. 64-5.
[3] *Autobiography*, Everyman Edition, p. 34.
[4] *Reliquiae Baxterianae*, I, p. 89.

2.

ECONOMIC BACKGROUND OF THE ENGLISH REVOLUTION

(*a*) *The Land*

ENGLAND at the beginning of the seventeenth century was a predominantly agricultural country. The overwhelming mass of the population lived in the countryside, engaged either wholly or partially in producing foodstuffs or wool. For centuries English society had been feudal, made up of isolated local communities producing for their own consumption, with very little trade between them. But gradually from the fifteenth to the seventeenth centuries a change began to come over the structure of this agricultural community. The food and wool from the village began to sell far afield: the spinsters and the husbandmen were turned into commodity-producers for a national market.

In 1492, moreover, Christopher Columbus had discovered America. English merchants followed him there, and also penetrated overseas to India and Russia. As industry and commerce developed, as the overseas market for English cloth expanded, some areas ceased to be economically self-sufficient, and had to be fed and supplied with wool for their looms. So we get the beginnings of a specialised division of labour. In the south of England—then the economically advanced part of the country—different regions began to concentrate on producing particular commodities. Those who had money began to keep large flocks of sheep, to grow food for this wider market, either on their own estates or on leased land. And very well they did out of it, too. For prices were going up. Silver had been discovered in America and began to flow into Europe at a time when commerce was expanding and money relations between landlord and tenant, employer and workman, were replacing the old relations based on payment in goods or labour services. Prices rose all through the sixteenth century: between 1510 and 1580 food trebled in price in England, and textiles rose by 150 per cent. This had the same effect as an inflation in our day. Those with fixed incomes got poorer, those living by trade and production for the market grew richer. So the middle classes prospered, the high feudal aristocracy (including the King and the bishops) and the smaller peasantry and wage labourers grew relatively poorer, except for the few individuals from those classes who were lucky enough to get in on the racket.

There was another factor. In 1536-40, in what is called the Reformation, the monasteries of England had been dissolved and their property confiscated. This was part of the struggle by which the national independence of England was established against the power and exploitation of the Catholic Church, and so was enthusiastically supported by the bourgeoisie and Parliament. Nor did they do badly out of it, for a great quantity of valuable and hitherto inaccessible land confiscated from the Church was thrown on to the market.

All these happenings were changing the structure of English rural society. Land was becoming a highly attractive field for investment of capital. People who had money wanted to buy land with it, and there were more and more people with money. In feudal England land had passed by inheritance from father to son, cultivated all the time in traditional ways for the consumption of one family; it had changed hands comparatively rarely. But now, the law adapting itself to the economic needs of society, land was beginning to become a commodity, bought and sold in a competitive market, and thus capital heaped up in the towns spilt over into the countryside.

The northern and western parts of England remained relatively untouched by the new commercial spirit radiating from London and the ports; but in the south and east many landowners were beginning to exploit their estates in a new way. Both in the Middle Ages and in the seventeenth century the first importance of an estate was that it supplied a landowner (through his control over the labour of others) with the means of livelihood. But over and above this, the large estates had in the Middle Ages maintained with their surplus agricultural produce a body of retainers who would on occasion act as soldiers, and so were the basis of the political power of the feudal lords. Now, with the development of the capitalist mode of production within the structure of feudalism, many landowners began either to market that portion of the produce of their estates which was not consumed by their families, or to lease their lands to a farmer who would produce for the market. So landowners came to regard their estates in a new light: as a source of money profit, of profits that were elastic and could be increased. Rents used to be fixed at levels maintained so long that they came to be regarded as "customary," as having existed "from time immemorial"; so did the many extortionate legal charges which feudal landowners extracted from the peasantry; but now they were being "racked up" to fantastically high levels. This was in itself a moral as well as an economic revolution, a break with all that men had held right and proper, and had the most disturbing effects on ways of thought and belief.

Codes of morals are always bound up with a given social order. Feudal society had been dominated by custom, tradition. Money had been comparatively unimportant. It was an outrage to the morals of such a society that men's rents should be sharply raised, and that if they could not pay, they should be turned out on the roads to beg, steal or starve. In time, the needs of growing capitalism produced a new morality—the morality of "God helps those who help themselves." But in the sixteenth century the idea that profit was more important than human life, so familiar to us that we have lost our sense of moral indignation, was very new and very shocking.

> "Is not he a greater thief," wrote the Puritan moralist, Stubbes, "that robbeth a man of his good name for ever, that taketh a man's house over his head, before his years be expired, that wresteth from a man his goods, his lands and livings . . . than he that stealeth a sheep, a cow, or

an ox, for necessity's sake only, having not otherwise to relieve his need?"[1]

But what did moral problems matter to the new type of landowners and lessees? They forced their incomes up to meet the rise in the prices of the goods they had to buy. They were able to evict tenants unable to pay the new rents, whose small holdings, perhaps, stood in the way of consolidating an estate into a large compact block for profitable sheep-farming on a large scale. Often rents were raised because the estate itself had been bought or leased at the competitive prices prevailing in the land market. And then the speculative purchaser or lessee wanted to get back in profits the capital he had laid out in his purchase money, in equipment and in improved methods of cultivation.

A new kind of farmer was thus emerging in the Home Counties—the capitalist farmer. He might be a pirate or a slave-trader, a respectable City merchant who had done well in currants or a country clothing capitalist. In any case he was looking for a safe investment for his profits, and one that would at the same time give him social standing.

For landowners controlled local government, as lords of manors or as justices of the peace. Only gentlemen were elected by their fellow landowners to represent the county in Parliament. The boroughs, too, came more and more to be represented in the House of Commons by a neighbouring gentleman. But the new farmer might be a feudal lord drawn by the pull of a near-by market and able to raise capital to reorganise the management of his estates; or he might be a lessee from the richer stratum of the peasantry.

Many of the latter class—the yeomen—were able by their wealth and ability to keep possession of their plots of land, to extend and consolidate them, to share in the new opportunities offered where they had access to a market. In the sixteenth century numbers of yeomen and gentlemen were consolidating their scattered strips of land, converting unenclosed arable to pasture or increasing their output of corn, fruit, vegetables, dairy produce for the town market. They were changing

[1] P. Stubbes, *Anatomy of Abuses*, ed. Furnivall, Part II, p. 14.

2

old-established tenures—turning copyholds into leaseholds, letting their lands for shorter periods—and ruthlessly evicting tenants unable to pay the new economic rents demanded.[1]

By all these means they enriched themselves in the same way as merchants and industrialists in the towns, and a class earning its wealth in a new way came to occupy a predominant position in some counties of southern and eastern England. This class was the basis of the famous squirearchy which was to govern England for the next three centuries.

But they did not have things all their own way before 1640. The structure of society was still essentially feudal; so were its laws and its political institutions. There were still many legal restrictions on the full unhampered capitalist utilisation of landed property, on free trade in land. These restrictions were maintained in the interests of the Crown, the feudal landowning class, and to a lesser extent, of the peasantry, anxious to live in the old secure way paying the old fixed dues. This legal network had to be broken through if rural capitalism was to develop the resources of the countryside to the full.

Bad communications still prevented the full development of a national market, restricted the possibilities of division of labour and so of capitalist developments in agriculture. So there still persisted in many parts even of the south and east, and all over northern and western England, landowners who lacked either the ability, the capital, the psychology or the opportunity to exploit their estates in the new way. They were still attempting to maintain feudal pomp and ceremony, still running their estates in the traditional way. Their courts were thronged with blue-blooded hangers-on, poor relations and retainers, who performed no productive functions in society, but still believed that the world owed them a living—"Drones" was what the bourgeois pamphleteers called them, as they had

[1] Copyholds were the normal peasant holdings, usually hereditary. The copyholder held by "the custom of the manor," was enrolled as occupier in the legal documents of the manor court. His right to possession was not always recognised by the common law courts. One of the great struggles of the sixteenth and seventeenth centuries was that in which copyholders strove to win full legal security for their tenures, whilst lords of manors (landlords) strove to render their possession uncertain and to keep it subject to decision in the manor court, presided over by the lord of the manor or his steward.

called the monks before them: "needless and disorderly attendants, old captains, old courtiers, unuseful scholars, and companions" was the unflattering description given by an astute steward of one of these large estates.[1]

The focus of this society was the King's Court. The largest landowner of this kind was the Crown itself, always short of capital. The bishops also were notoriously easy-going landowners, whose estates were developed, if at all, by lessees. A contemporary observed that " they never raise nor rack their rents as the noblemen and gentlemen do to the uttermost penny, but do let their lands as they were let a hundred years since".[2]

Times were hard for these parasites and *rentiers*. The rise in prices made it impossible for them to keep up their old standards of living, still less to compete in luxury with the merchant princes. They were continually in debt, often to some smart city business man who demanded a mortgage on their estate, and stepped into it when the debt fell due. The needy courtier, the proud but penniless younger son of a noble house, were commonplaces of popular derision and middle-class contempt. Yet this class was still a social and political power; the State was organised to safeguard its interests. Its inability to reorganise its estates was keeping a large amount of capital uninvested. Much of the richest land in England was not utilised to the full technical capacities of the time.[3] State power was being used to *prevent* the growth of a national market.

There was an acute struggle of all classes to profit by the agricultural changes taking place. In general they made for greater productivity, and enabled some richer peasants and small landowners to rise in the world. But for many smaller

[1] J. Smyth, *Lives of the Berkeleys*, Vol. II, p. 114.

[2] Sir Thomas Wilson, *The State of England, 1600*, ed. F. J. Fisher, Camden Miscellany, XVI, pp. 22-3.

[3] A similar situation exists under capitalism at the present time, where big monopoly concerns buy up inventions in order to prevent them being used, and where food is destroyed whilst millions go hungry. The seventeenth-century English revolution by transferring State power to the bourgeoisie made possible the full development of all the resources of English society in the eighteenth century. A transition to socialism will be necessary to win the same result in England to-day.

cultivators they meant depression, the raising of rents and dues of various kinds, the enclosure of the common fields on which the villagers had for centuries pastured their cattle and geese. Many husbandmen whose small properties stood in the way of a farmer wanting to consolidate a large sheep farm were brutally evicted.

> "Your sheep," wrote Sir Thomas More in the early sixteenth century, "that were wont to be so meek and tame, and so small eaters, now, as I hear say, be become so great devourers and so wild, that they eat up and swallow down the very men themselves."[1]
>
> "The psychology of landowning had been revolutionised," Professor Tawney sums up, "and for two generations the sharp landlord, instead of using his seigneurial right to fine or arrest runaways from the villein nest, had been hunting for flaws in titles, screwing up admission fines, twisting manorial customs, and, when he dared, turning copyholds into leases."[2]

Or, as Philip Stubbes put it: "Landlords make merchandise of their poor tenants."

Against this treatment revolt smouldered throughout the period; it broke out in open rebellion in 1549, 1607 and 1631, but each time the peasantry was beaten back into submission. The State is always an instrument of coercion in the hands of the ruling class; and landlords ruled sixteenth-century England. Some of these poor tenants became vagabonds wandering the roads for bread, so laws were passed ordering vagrants to be branded or to be "whipped until his or her shoulders be bloody." "The fathers of the present working-class," as Marx puts it in *Capital*, "were chastised for their enforced transformation into vagabonds and paupers. Legislation treated them as 'voluntary' criminals."[3] Others became agricultural labourers working on the large estates. Others again provided a useful supply of cheap labour for expanding industries. Both these groups were without land

[1] *Utopia*, Everyman Edition, p. 23.
[2] Tawney, *Religion and the Rise of Capitalism*, Penguin Edition, p. 139.
[3] Marx, *Capital*, Vol. I, ed. Dona Torr, p. 758.

to support them in independence in a bad year or when their employers went bankrupt. They were on their way to becoming proletarians, with nothing to offer in the market but their labour, at the mercy of all the fluctuations and insecurity of capitalism.

> "Thus," to quote Marx again, "thus were the agricultural people, firstly forcibly expropriated from the soil, driven from their homes, turned into vagabonds, and then whipped, branded, tortured by laws grotesquely terrible, into the discipline necessary for the wage system."[1]

We must be careful, however, not to antedate these developments, nor to exaggerate their extent: they are significant as the dominant tendency. Similarly the new progressive landowners and farmers catch the eye as the rising and expanding class perhaps more than could be justified statistically. The improving landlord was not typical before 1660.

And we must remember what the agricultural changes in pre-revolutionary England were. They took place within a given system of technical equipment. There was no large-scale revolution in agricultural *technique* till the eighteenth century, though its first beginnings can be traced back to the revolutionary decades of the seventeenth century. The changes of the period before 1640, which were enormously accelerated in the years between 1640 and 1660, were changes in landownership, and in the volume of production rather than in the technique of production. So the changes had no revolutionary effect on society as a whole. The new class of capitalist farmers was there, thrusting its way forward, hampered by feudal survivals, without whose abolition it could not develop freely; in the revolution, in alliance with the urban bourgeoisie, it took over the State, creating the conditions within which further expansion was possible.

On the other hand, not only did large areas in the north and west remain unaffected by the new changes, but even where these changes were taking place large sections of the peasantry still survived in 1640 as semi-independent cultivators. This important group found itself in temporary alliance with

[1] *Ibid.*, p. 761.

the dominant bourgeois forces in opposition to a Crown which did little to help it; but when it discovered, as it did after 1647, what the real aims of its allies were, it began to fight, in company with other radical elements, to push the revolution leftwards. But because its instincts and social aims were to some extent pre-capitalist, looking backward to a stable peasant community, it was bound to be defeated. The current is one which cannot be ignored because it explains why in Puritan social ideas and Leveller[1] social aims there is a trend that is " mediæval" and even reactionary.

(*b*) *Industry and Trade*

Though most English people before 1640 worked in the fields, changes no less important than those we have described were taking place in trade and industry, changes, indeed, which gave the impetus to the agrarian developments. Something like an industrial revolution took place in the century before 1640, stimulated by capital liberated at the dissolution and plunder of the monasteries, or acquired by trade, piracy and plunder from the New World or by the slave trade. England had long been a great wool-growing country, exporting raw material to the Netherlands to be worked up into cloth. Now the English clothing industry developed with great rapidity, and English merchants began to export finished or semi-finished cloths on a far larger scale. At the same time a great development took place in coal-mining; by 1640 England produced over four-fifths of the coal of Europe. Coal played a prominent part in the growth of very many other industries—iron, tin, glass, soap, shipbuilding.

This industrial boom caused a great expansion in the volume of England's trade, and the switch-over from export of raw materials to finished products caused a change in its direction too. England ceased to be merely a source of raw materials for the west European countries, began to compete with their manufactures and so to reach further afield for markets, raw materials and luxury imports—to Russia, Turkey,

[1] The Levellers were the left wing of the revolutionaries. Who they were and what their aims were is discussed below.

the East and West Indies. Hence the beginnings of English colonisation, in order to develop trade and to win monopoly political control over the parts of the world which England was aiming to exploit economically. This called for a stronger State machine and led to the rise of English sea-power in order to challenge Spain, the great colonial power.

The defeat of the Spanish Armada in 1588 gave English overseas commerce the chance to develop freely. On the other hand, it made the bourgeoisie in England more acutely aware of the restrictions checking their expansion at home. Parliament began to attack the monarchy and its attempt to regulate the economic life of the country from the moment when the defeat of the Armada created a feeling of political security. (We must not exaggerate the *extent* of this development before 1640, because it was hampered by many obstructions, as we shall see: but the *tendency* is clear.)

These new economic developments created new class conflicts. Capital for industrial development was supplied, directly or indirectly, by merchants, slave-traders and pirates, who had amassed fortunes overseas, and by that section of the gentry which had made its fortune in the plunder of the monasteries and in the new agriculture; it was also being accumulated by the savings of yeomen and craftsmen.

From the start the merchants, organised in companies, controlled export, as they had done throughout the Middle Ages; merchant middlemen dominated internal trade. The factory system had not yet developed; the "putting-out" system, by which wool or yarn was supplied by the merchant to be spun or woven by the labourer and his family in his own home (also called the "domestic system"), meant that even if the producer sometimes owned the instruments of production—spinning-wheel or loom—he was completely dependent on his employer for supplies and so for his income. In bad periods he was continually falling into debt, usually to the capitalist who employed him. In this way, vast fortunes were made by employers and usurers at the expense of small proprietors.

Occasionally, indeed, a small master managed to "better himself" by fortunate borrowing of the capital which was indispensable if one was to get on, but far more were unlucky. Hence the small producers joined in the clamour of the feudal landlords against "usury." They could not do without loans, and yet were crippled by the high rates of interest which could be exacted in a pre-capitalist society. "Usury" was to ordinary people what wage-labour is to their successors to-day. The employer exploited his workman under the domestic system by charging him high prices and high rates of interest even more than by paying him low wages. Hence there was coming into existence a petty-bourgeois class with specific economic interests of its own, but changing in composition as its most enterprising and lucky members rose to become capitalists, and the unfortunate sank to be wage-labourers. The strongholds of this class were East Anglia and the south Midlands, later to be the centres of the most uncompromising resistance to Charles I.

There were as many and as serious obstacles to the expansion of capitalism in trade and industry as in agriculture. During the Middle Ages trade and industry had been restricted to the towns, where they had been rigidly controlled by the gilds. These were associations of producers who established a monopoly over the local market and kept it by restricting output and competition, regulating prices and quality of production, controlling their apprentices and journeymen. (Under the apprentice system an artisan had to undergo seven years' training before being allowed to set up on his own.) This system presupposed a static and closed local market; feudal economic theory was based on the idea of a comparatively stable society.

But now the market was expanding: the whole nation was becoming one economic unit. Capital sought profits by investment in any economic activity, and the capitalist was not interested in knowing where his products were sold, provided they sold at a profit. The local barriers to trade broke down. The market town could no longer bully the surrounding countryside, for it had to face the competition of merchants from London, peddling their wares and buying up the products of local handicrafts. Competition broke up monopoly. For overseas trade, indeed, merchants still found it advantageous to join together in companies for self-defence in distant lands and unpoliced seas: in those days many a merchant was a pirate in his spare time. The Tudor State was able to keep some control over these companies by selling them its protection and generous charters of privileges.

But it was very different in industry. The high standards of quality of the town craft gilds, their restrictions on competition and output, became in the eyes of capitalist entrepreneurs so many stupid obstacles to free production, preventing them meeting the demands of the expanding market. To escape from these shackles, industry overflowed from the boroughs to the suburbs and unincorporated towns and countryside, where production was free from interference and regulation. Here they found a supply of cheap labour in the peasantry ruined and expropriated by the agricultural changes. Many of the new industries—e.g. coal and alum mining—were almost entirely capitalist from the start. Nevertheless, the corporate towns still tried to monopolise local trade, to make their markets a bottle-neck through which all commodities must flow.

The merchant middlemen, on the other hand, were trying to meet the demands of the London and export markets by dealing direct with the producer (e.g. of food). So they came into conflict with the market regulations of the corporate towns and their reactionary oligarchies. Their privileges and restrictions, and the apprentice system, remained as a serious check to the full development of the productive resources of the country, to the free flow of capital into industry. The gilds were so many vested interests linked up with the social structure of feudalism, opposed to the newer, freer forces of capitalism.

As the old industrial control broke down, the Crown, in the interests of the feudal landowning class (and a small court group of financiers and racketeers), tried to impose new controls. Monopolies—the sale to a particular individual of exclusive rights of production and/or sale of a particular commodity (or the exclusive right to trade in a particular overseas market)—were the means by which the Crown tried to bring industry and trade under control, on a national scale now that the town gilds had been circumvented. We shall see how this attempt failed, and the disastrous results of its failure for the monarchy.

It can be realised how this vast industrial and commercial expansion reacted on agriculture and landholding: for the agrarian changes were caused in part by the demand for more food to feed the new urban areas, in part by the demand for wool for the expanding clothing industry, or by the hunt for minerals; in each case the needs of the merchant class were identical with those of the capitalist farmers and progressive landowners. And the migration of capital to the countryside, whether by the leasing or purchase of estates or by loans, brought a new business and competitive spirit into the hitherto relatively static and traditional agrarian relations. Where the families of tenant and landlord had for centuries occupied their respective estates, the tenant paying a non-economic rent[1], relations were very different from those existing between a new purchaser and a capitalist lessee.

The point to be stressed is this. There was a great deal of capital in England which merchants, yeomen and gentlemen were anxious to invest in the freest possible industrial, commercial and agricultural development. This was continually thwarted by feudal survivals in town and country, and by government policy deliberately endeavouring in the interests of the old landed ruling class to restrict production and the accumulation of capital. Thus, in attacking the feudal landlords' state and the oligarchy of big merchants in alliance with the Court who were trying to monopolise business profits, the struggle of the bourgeoisie was progressive, representing the interests of the country as a whole.

England in 1640 was still ruled by landlords and the relations of production were still partly feudal, but there was this vast and expanding capitalist sector, whose development the Crown and feudal landlords could not for ever hold in check. There

[1] I.e. a rent which did not correspond to the price now obtainable for the land. The landlord could make more by leasing his lands at rack-rent than by himself receiving the services, dues in kind, etc., supplied by customary tenants. So security of tenure, if copyholders could have won it, would have been an obstacle to the development of large-scale capitalist agriculture (see p. 18, n.).

were few proletarians (except in London), most of the producers under the putting-out system being also small peasants. But these peasants and small artisans were losing their independence. They were hit especially hard by the general rise in prices, and were being brought into ever closer dependence on the merchants and squires. A statute of 1563 forbad the poorer 75 per cent. of the rural population to go as apprentices into industry.

So there were really three classes in conflict. As against the parasitic feudal landowners and speculative financiers, as against the government whose policy was to restrict and control industrial expansion, the interests of the new class of capitalist merchants and farmers were temporarily identical with those of the small peasantry and artisans and journeymen. But conflict between the two latter classes was bound to develop, since the expansion of capitalism involved the dissolution of the old agrarian and industrial relationships and the transformation of independent small masters and peasants into proletarians.

3.

POLITICAL BACKGROUND OF THE ENGLISH REVOLUTION

(a) *The Tudor monarchy*

SET against this background of economic and social transition, the role of the Tudor monarchy becomes clear. Itself rooted in feudal society, it could to a certain extent balance between the bourgeoisie and progressive gentry, on the one hand, and the feudal lords on the other. After the great noble houses had destroyed one another in the fifteenth-century Wars of the Roses, the strength of the advancing and declining classes was in equilibrium for a brief period, during which the function of the monarchy was to see that concessions to bourgeois demands did the least possible harm to the ruling class. The merchants wished for a united England, orderly and policed, with uniform laws, weights and measures: Henry VII and his successors saw to it that this unity centred around the person of the King, that the policing was done by the country gentry (J.Ps.). The bourgeoisie attacked the Church for its wealth and unproductiveness; Henry VIII led the "reformation" of 1529-40, and saw to it that the political power and a part of the wealth of the Church passed to the Crown. Most of the monastic estates went ultimately to those who had money to buy them, and so strengthened the new element in the countryside. Queen Mary succeeded in re-establishing Catholicism for a few years, but could not get the monastic estates back out of the clutches of their purchasers. Similarly, the Crown tried to control trade and industry in the interests of the national exchequer, posed frequently as the defender of the peasant and artisan against the rich: but always in the last resort it continued to retreat before the bourgeoisie, on whom it depended for supplies and loans.

In fact, until about 1590, the monarchy had many interests in common with those of the bourgeoisie in town and country —in the struggle against Spain, against the international Catholic Church, against rival noble houses disputing supreme control with the House of Tudor and ruining the country with their private wars. Hence the collaboration in Parliament between monarchy, gentry and bourgeoisie. Yet there was a point beyond which the retreat could not be continued, and ultimately the unity of interest broke down.

Up to a point, indeed, the bourgeoisie and the feudal gentry were able to get along together under the monarchy. In an age when plunder and piracy helped in the rapid accumulation of capital, the reckless seadogs of the semi-feudal south-western counties—Devon and Cornwall—heaped up wealth on a scale which the more cautious merchants of London could never have imitated. In looting Spanish colonies and Spanish treasure ships for gold, in the quest for land in Ireland and North America, the adventurers of the decaying class did not come into conflict with the rising entrepreneurs. Those who were fortunate acquired the capital necessary to take part in production for the market themselves: the lines of class division had not yet crystallised.

This hardening process took place in the reigns of James I and Charles I. By then the new landed gentry and respectable traders wished to settle down to peaceful development and legitimate trade. "The new age had turned its back on the gold which did not come through chartered companies."[1] "Peace and law have beggared us all," wailed the future royalist Sir John Oglander.[2]

So the feudal gentry, as their incomes from land declined, became more and more dependent on the court for jobs and economic pickings, more and more parasitic. As the Stuart monarchy became progressively less useful to the bourgeoisie, so it became more indispensable to the aristocracy and courtiers, their only guarantee of economic survival. That is why they were to fight for it so desperately in the Civil War.

For the monarchy was bound up with the feudal order by more than the bonds of conservative sentiment. The King was himself the greatest of feudal landlords and, though he was in a better position than others to get a rake-off from the new capitalist wealth, he was opposed no less than any other landowner to a fundamental change from a feudal to a capitalist order of society.

In the early sixteenth century the monarchy had used the bourgeoisie as an ally against its most powerful rivals—the other great feudal houses weakened by the Wars of the Roses and the Church. The alliance between Crown and Parliament (representing the landed classes and the merchants) had in the early sixteenth century been genuine. The new men prospered under the shelter of the throne; the monarchy defended them from internal reaction or revolt, as when it defeated the Pilgrimage of Grace (1536) and the rising of the northern earls (1569). The Crown also defended them from the external reactionary power of Spain (the Armada). The only time when reaction seemed for a brief period likely to triumph was when Queen Mary was married to Philip of Spain; and then the terror and burnings with which alone her policy could be

[1] D. Matthew, *The Jacobean Age*, p. 16.
[2] Bamford, *A Royalist's Notebook*, p. 13.

carried through helped to confirm the national hatred of Catholicism. So the collaboration between Crown and Parliament in the Tudor period was based on a community of real interests. The Parliamentary franchise was very restricted and the House of Commons represented exclusively the landed class and the merchants, whilst the House of Lords remained the more important chamber until the Commons seized the initiative in James I's reign. Parliament under the Tudors did not meet often, and then normally approved the royal policy.

But by the last decade of the sixteenth century, when all its internal and external foes had been crushed, the bourgeoisie ceased to depend on the protection of the monarchy; at the same time the Crown became increasingly aware of the dangerous possibilities of the growing wealth of the bourgeoisie, and strove to consolidate its position before it was too late.

This clash can be seen in the quarrels of James I and Charles I with their Parliaments. The change was in the relative strength of the class forces; James was sillier than Elizabeth, but this alone does not account for the failure of his policy where hers succeeded. James formulated grandiose theories of the divine right of kings where Elizabeth had preserved a prudent silence; but this is a symptom of the growing divergence between Crown and Parliament, not a cause. James had to define his position because it was being called in question. The real crux of the problem was finance, over which there had already been conflict at the end of Elizabeth's reign. Prices were rising, the wealth of the bourgeoisie was increasing by leaps and bounds, yet the revenue of the Crown, as of most great landowners, remained static and inadequate to the new needs. Unless the Crown could tap the new wealth either (*a*) by drastically increasing taxation at the expense of the bourgeoisie and gentry, or (*b*) by somehow taking part in the productive process itself, its independent power must disappear.

The first policy—increased customs, forced loans, new taxes—led to violent quarrels with Parliament, which had long claimed the right to control taxation, and was not going to allow taxes to be increased unless it was given full control over the machinery of State.

The second policy led to the erection of monopolies in the attempt to control certain industries and obtain a *rentier's* rake-off from that control, e.g. coal, alum, soap, etc. It outraged the whole business population, capitalists and employees alike. The scandal reached its height in "Cockayne's project" (1616). This was a scheme to bring the clothing industry under royal control and expand exports to the advantage of the Exchequer. It was sabotaged by the exporters, and led to a crisis of over-production and widespread unemployment, the blame for which attached itself to the Crown.

A third policy, tried by the Stuarts after all others had failed, never had a chance of success. This was an attempt to revive and increase the revenue from feudal dues. There was no chance of the Crown becoming financially independent of the bourgeoisie from this source alone; the only consequence of its exploitation was the alienation of the Crown's potential friends among the aristocracy and gentry, as well as of the bourgeoisie. For with the increasing economic difficulties, and the political threat from the bourgeoisie, the monarchy was thrown back on the exclusive support of the nobility and the economically unprogressive, parasitic elements in the state. On the other side, the nobility itself came to depend more and more on the Crown's control of economic life to maintain its own position. It wanted Court patronage for its landless younger sons, whom bourgeois competition was driving out of the professions; it wanted privileges and monopolies which would give it a *rentier's* share in the profits of developing capitalism. It is not surprising that the major parliamentary clashes of the early seventeenth century were over this very issue of monopolies. They were the means by which the monarchy attempted to control and canalise commercial activity in the interests of the greedy courtiers, the "drones," in denunciation of whom Puritan sermons abounded.

Another great landowner remains to be considered, whose interests were even more closely bound up with those of the monarchy—the Church hierarchy. Since the dissolution of the monasteries, the remaining possessions of the Church of England were coveted by a section of the gentry. Only the usefulness of the bishops to the Crown protected the Church from further spoliation. Its moral authority, too, could now no longer be drawn from the international Papacy with which Henry VIII had broken, but came from the national monarchy, its only defender against Catholic reaction and left-wing Protestant revolutionaries. So the Elizabethan Church stood for passive obedience to divinely constituted authority, and preached that rebellion was the worst possible sin. The dependence of the Church on the Crown was a century old by 1640, and their alliance was based on the closest community of interest. As the breach between Crown and bourgeoisie widened, so the Puritan attack on the Church, on its forms and ceremonies, its courts and discipline, became hardly distinguishable from the Parliamentary attack on the Crown. A group of merchants in London formed a society for establishing lectureships in the "barren parts" of the country, and lecturers nominated by town corporations incurred the special hostility of Charles I's Archbishop, Laud, who rightly suspected that their theology and political theory would be equally "unsound" from the point of view of the Government.

Two social systems and their ideologies were in conflict. Presbyterianism (which advocated abolition of the royally appointed bishops and the domination of each Church by elders—local bigwigs) was an oligarchical theory which especially appealed to the big bourgeoisie. What they wanted was a Church organised in such a way as to be capable of diffusing throughout the whole of society the political and economic ways of thinking convenient for the merchant class. For it has been abundantly demonstrated how the morality that Puritanism preached was precisely the outlook needed for the accumulation of capital and expansion of capitalism. The emphasis was on thrift, sobriety, hard work in the station to which God had called a man; on unceasing labour in whatever calling, merchant or artisan, one happened to be, but with no extravagant enjoyment of the fruits of labour, and unceasing preoccupation with duty to the detriment of "worldly" pleasure. The wealthy were to accumulate capital, the poor to labour at their tasks—as a divine duty and always under the "great Task-master's" eye. This belief inspired the bourgeoisie to remodel society in the divinely ordained fashion as God's "elect," and if that fashion bore a striking resemblance to the capitalist system, they were ever more fervently convinced that they were doing the work of God and that ultimate victory was both predestined and assured. Their conviction of "salvation" was born of the historical necessity and progressiveness of their task, and was confirmed by the material prosperity with which God tended to bless his servants.

The hierarchy counter-attacked by trying to increase tithe payments in the towns, and to recover some of the Church's lost revenues (tithes which had been "impropriated"—that is to say, diverted into the pockets of a lay landlord from the ecclesiastical purposes for which they had originally been charged on all occupiers of property). At the same time, it tried to extend its control over patronage, in order to appoint to Church livings socially and doctrinally satisfactory incumbents. "Subversive" views on doctrine and discipline were ruthlessly punished by the ecclesiastical Court of High Commission, with Laud at its head. The Puritan opposition depicted the whole trend of Charles's policy as a return to papistry, which is truer in spirit than in the letter. Laud was no doctrinal papist, and he refused all overtures from Rome; but the social policy which he personified was an attempt to revive and perpetuate obsolete mediæval economic and social relations and the ways of thinking corresponding to them. Thus the fight to control the Church was of fundamental importance; whoever controlled its doctrine and organisation was in a position to determine the nature of society. James I was making a shrewd political analysis when he said, "No Bishop, no King." It was only three years after the abolition of episcopacy that Charles I died on the scaffold.

(*b*) *Resistance to the Stuarts*

The political struggle was waged in Parliament during the early years of the century. It covered many subjects—religious, economic, constitutional. With religion were confused questions of foreign policy. Since the war against the reactionary power of Spain and the defeat of the Armada, English Protestantism and English patriotism were closely connected.

James outraged them both when, through fear of the revolutionary tendencies of extreme Protestantism in England and abroad, he drew closer to Spain. For many years the Spanish Ambassador Gondomar was the chief influence at James's Court, the best-hated man in England; and during those years Spanish diplomacy and Spanish armies advanced at the cost of Protestants all over the Continent. The bourgeoisie knew its friends. Against James's policy of appeasement, the House of Commons called for a militant anti-Spanish policy. But this was only to be secured after the downfall of the monarchy. Its foreign policy reflected the interests of reaction in England and Europe, and a fundamental reversal of foreign policy is possible only by means of a fundamental change in the social system.

Meanwhile, in consequence, great opportunities for English expansion in the New World were lost; the carrying trade of Europe, for want of a forward policy, was lost to the bourgeois Dutch Republic, and English cloth was driven from German markets. Even where the Crown pursued a colonising policy and tried to enlist the support of the bourgeoisie—in Ireland—there were two divergent views on colonisation. James I envisaged the City's Londonderry Company as merely Government agents, whose job was to provide yeomen settlers to defend and police the conquered and occupied districts, whereas the City merchants wished to retain the "native Irish" as a source of cheap labour for absentee employers. The royal and feudalist conception of colonisation—emphasising strategic and policing considerations and the need for land for the impoverished gentry—clashed with the bourgeois vision of colonies as a source of steady profits. Charles I even further alienated the City by revoking the company's charter after £50,000 capital had been lost, and imposing a fine of £70,000 (ultimately reduced to £12,000) merely because the citizens had put profit before the letter of their obligations. (This, like other fines, was a useful windfall for the Government at the time, but did not make it much easier for the Crown subsequently to raise loans in the City. The fact that "there were no safe investments under the *ancien régime*" is always given as one of the causes of the French Revolution.)

The later ruthless determination of the bourgeoisie to subjugate Ireland, leading up to Cromwell's conquest in 1649, dates back to the losses over the Londonderry plantation.

Foreign policy is linked with finance as well as with religion. James claimed that his weak foreign policy was due to lack of money, at a time when the bourgeoisie was becoming visibly richer. But there could be no financial concessions to a government which the moneyed classes did not trust. Over James's and Charles's attempts to replenish the Exchequer there were many clashes. Imports were taxed without consent of Parliament ("impositions"). Monopolies aimed at tapping industrial profits, and were declared illegal by Parliament. "Cockayne's project" for control of the export of cloth was an attempt at State interference with the processes of production. Its failure caused a grave economic crisis, and led in 1621 to the first large-scale denunciation of the whole economic policy of the Government and the surrender of James on that issue. Charles, who succeeded his father in 1625, used forced loans, backed up by arbitrary arrest of those who refused to pay (the Five Knights' Case).

This led to an open breach. In the Petition of Right, 1628, Parliament declared that taxation without its consent and arbitrary arrest were alike illegal; other clauses tried to make it impossible for the King to maintain a standing army. For that was clearly the direction in which the Government was tending. Charles accepted the Petition of Right perforce, but then immediately quarrelled with the Commons over its interpretation. In March, 1629, Parliament was dissolved by a sudden coup, but not before a violent scene in the Lower House in which resolutions were passed, aiming at making it impossible for the King to get in any revenue, and casting suspicion on his whole policy as "papist" and in the interest of foreign Powers.

The point had been reached beyond which the King could retreat no further without virtual abdication to the bourgeoisie. The situation was already revolutionary, but Charles had taken the initiative, and for eleven years he was able to try his hand at personal government. His ministers were not inefficient. There was Archbishop Laud in London. Sir

Thomas Wentworth, leader of the Yorkshire gentry as opposed to the clothing interest in that county, whose compromising leadership had been rejected by the House of Commons in 1628, now came over openly to the King's side. He was made President of the Council in the North, later Lord Lieutenant of Ireland and Earl of Strafford. In Ireland he distinguished himself by brutal efficiency, and built up a powerful and papist army which struck terror into the hearts of English parliamentarians. The opposition was temporarily driven underground.

During these years England was at peace with the world, so the experiment of personal government was carried out under the most favourable circumstances. Yet Charles's system proved a total failure, and broke down of its own accord. The Government alienated all sections of the community. It annoyed the common lawyers by interfering with the judges to get the sort of legal decisions it wanted (James I had been guilty of this, too) and by relying on the prerogative courts (Star Chamber, Council in the North and in Wales) as instruments of policy.

These courts had been used by the Tudors, partly to deal with commercial causes which the common law was not competent to handle, partly to suppress feudal anarchy and maintain the order so necessary to a commercial civilisation. But during the Tudor period the common law—product of a feudal society—had adapted itself to the needs of the business world, its personnel had come to be drawn largely from the bourgeoisie; and now that the dangers from baronial disorder no longer existed, the wide executive powers of the prerogative courts were looked upon with fear by the bourgeoisie, who no longer needed their protection and might become their victims. The judges in the Star Chamber were for all practical purposes almost identical with the Government in the Privy Council.

The bourgeoisie thus found willing allies in the lawyers, anxious for their fees, as well as in all those who detested the methods of the prerogative courts. The cutting off of Prynne's ears for writing a pamphlet which the Government held to have slighted the Queen, the flogging of Lilburne for distributing illegal literature, made the Government's victims popular heroes.

The financial expedients of Charles's personal Government affected all classes. Feudal dues were revived and extended, and that hit landlords and their tenants. The decline of the Navy and attacks of pirates on shipping and coast towns were made the excuse for collecting ship-money. This was an obsolete national tax not voted by Parliament, falling especially on the towns and the gentry. Monopolies and the tightened grip of corrupt Court circles on the economic life of the country meant wealth for a few big merchants, but grave inconvenience for the vast mass of business men and small producers.

Monopolies were the most uneconomical form of taxation. It has been estimated that whereas every 6*s*. charged to the consumer by the Customs brought 5*s*. into the Exchequer, 6*s*. increased cost to the consumer in monopolies brought about 10*d*. into the Exchequer. The rest went to the privileged group of Court parasites, who fulfilled no productive function themselves and were an enormous drag on the full development of the productive capacities of the country.[1] The soap monopoly severely hampered the woollen industry. The salt monopoly hit fish-curing. All industries suffered from a rise in the price of coal due to the Crown's alliance with a ring of exporters. Monopolies caused a sharp rise in prices all round, which hit the poor especially hard. There were monopolies (and therefore increased prices) on necessities, such as butter, herrings, salt, beer, soap and too many others to enumerate. "Is not bread there?" an indignant Member of Parliament demanded when the list was read out in 1601.

In face of these facts, the manœuvres of the Government to enlist the support of the poorer peasants against their landlords deceived no one (except a recent school of reactionary historians[2]) and were not even effective. Commissions were set

[1] W. R. Scott, *Joint Stock Companies*, I, p. 221.

[2] They rely largely on the statement of the historian Clarendon that the period 1629-40 was one of great prosperity for the mass of the population. On this Thorold Rogers, the historian of prices, comments: "I am convinced, by comparison of wages, rents and prices, that it was a period of excessive misery among the mass of the people and the tenants, a time in which a few might have become rich, while the many were crushed

up to punish landlords whose enclosures had led to eviction, but the financial extremity of the Government was such that it could never resist the offers of rich men to buy themselves off. There were many people of admirable intentions in Charles's Government, but they were unable to make anything of the rotten system they were trying to work. This is especially clear in the case of Laud, whose views on the need for beauty and uniformity in church worship led him to violent persecution of his opponents, to espionage and the throttling down of all criticism. Thus all honest Puritans, and many who had no strong religious views at all, were driven willy-nilly into political opposition, and even such a long-established custom as the payment of tithes to the established Church began to be widely called in question.

During these eleven years the opposition was organising itself as well as growing. Its centre was a group of landed families, closely connected by trade and intermarriage, who were always well represented in both Houses of Parliament. The sort of State they wanted could not be procured without the overthrow of the Laud-Strafford régime (though there were as yet few republicans).

The first great signal of revolt was John Hampden's refusal to pay Ship Money in 1637, and his trial and condemnation focused attention in a way that the more cruel imprisonment of Eliot and other Parliamentary leaders in 1629 had failed to do. (Eliot died in prison, as the Government intended him to do. On one occasion the Lieutenant of the Tower was severely reprimanded for allowing air from an open window to reach this dangerous prisoner.)

The bourgeoisie thus saw that their economic grievances could only be redressed by political action; the royal economic policies, hitting the capitalist class as a whole, could not be improved by the winning of small privileges for particular

down into hopeless and almost permanent indigence" (*The Economic Interpretation of History*, p. 139). Clarendon is hardly an impartial witness, for he had been the chief Councillor of Charles I and Charles II in exile, and was Charles II's first Minister after the Restoration, until the Parliamentary opposition drove him out of the country again in 1667. Of course he wanted to boost the old régime. He is refuted by the contemporary despatches of the Venetian Ambassador.

members of the class. The demand for a business government, strong ever since the crisis of 1621, grew rapidly. Following Hampden's example, there was a general refusal to pay taxes in the years 1639-40. The bourgeoisie had gone on strike.

Meanwhile Charles's system had broken down at its weakest link—in Scotland. Scotland was a much more backward country than England economically, but politically the gentry had thrown off the control of Church, Crown and big aristocracy. Charles I wanted to reverse this achievement. His attempt to extend royal control over the Church of Scotland, and his threat to resume Church lands there, created a national revolt for which there was much sympathy in England. When a Scottish army invaded England in 1639, the absence of all popular support as well as sheer lack of means forced Charles to come to terms with it.

In the economic crisis of 1640 he was utterly bankrupt. He outraged commercial circles by seizing bullion deposited in the Tower and by proposing to debase the coinage. The State machine—which depended on the support of the middle-class J.Ps.—ceased to function. The Scots refused to leave England without an indemnity. The English army sent against them was mutinous and had to be paid. A Parliament could no longer be avoided. Even so Charles dissolved one Parliament after three weeks (the Short Parliament); but in November, 1640, the Long Parliament met, to which the Government had to surrender. Pym, Hampden and other Opposition leaders had stumped the country in a successful election campaign. They were helped by riots against enclosures in the countryside and by mass demonstrations in the City. The last time the rack was used in England was to torture a youth who had led a procession to Lambeth to hunt "William the Fox" (Archbishop Laud).

This Parliament differed from its predecessors only in the length of its session. It represented the same classes—principally the gentry and wealthy merchants. Consequently, it came to reflect the division among the English gentry corresponding roughly to the economic division between feudal north-west and capitalist south-east. But the House of Commons did not make the revolution: its members were subject to pressure from outside, from the people of London, the yeomen and artisans of the home counties.

But in 1640 most classes were united against the Crown. The final issues were: (*a*) destruction of the bureaucratic machinery whereby the Government had been able to rule in contravention of the desires of the great majority of its politically influential subjects (Strafford was executed, Laud imprisoned, other leading Ministers fled abroad; the Star Chamber, Court of High Commission, and other prerogative courts were abolished); (*b*) prevention of a standing army controlled by the King; (*c*) abolition of the recent financial expedients, whose aim had also been to render the King independent of the control of the bourgeoisie through Parliament, and whose effect had been economic dislocation and the undermining of confidence; (*d*) Parliamentary (i.e. bourgeois) control of the Church, so that it could no longer be used as a reactionary propaganda agency.

A crisis was forced by a revolt in Ireland in 1641. With the withdrawal of Strafford, the English Government there, which had long been oppressive, ceased to be strong, and the Irish seized the opportunity to attempt to throw off the English yoke. Parliament was united in its determination to keep the first British colony in subjection; but the bourgeoisie firmly refused to trust Charles with an army for its re-conquest (Royalist plots in the armed forces had already been exposed). So Parliament was reluctantly forced to take control of the Army.

The unanimity inside Parliament came to an end. To most of the aristocracy and conservative gentry, the policy of the leaders of the House of Commons, and especially their readiness to appeal to public opinion outside Parliament, seemed leading to a break-up of the social order in which their dominant position was secure, and they gradually fell back to support of the King. In the country as a whole, the division went along broad class lines. The landed class was divided, many being frightened by riots against enclosures and threats of a peasant revolt, such as had shaken the Midlands in 1607; the progressive section of the gentry and the bourgeoisie were confident that they could ride the storm. In London, whilst monopolists and the ruling oligarchy supported the court from which their profits came, the main body of merchants, artisans and apprentices gave active support to the forward party in Parliament, and pushed it steadily further along the revolutionary path. The great leader of the Commons, Pym, welcomed this popular support, and in the Grand Remonstrance (November, 1641) the revolutionary leaders drew up a sweeping indictment of Charles's Government, and published it for propaganda purposes—a new technique of appeal to the people.

But the decision to print the Remonstrance had been the occasion of a savage clash in the House and was passed by only eleven votes, after which the division became irreconcilable. The future Royalists withdrew from Parliament, not (as is often alleged) because of their devotion to bishops, but rather (as a Member said in the debate) because, "if we make a parity in the Church we must come to a parity in the Commonwealth." If the property of the ecclesiastical landlords could be confiscated, whose turn might not come next? The big bourgeoisie itself was frightened, and felt the need of some kind of monarchical settlement (with a reformed monarchy responsive to its interests) to check the flow of popular feeling. It tried desperately to stem the revolutionary torrent it had let loose. One gentleman switched over from the side of Parliament to the King because he feared that "the necessitous people of the whole kingdom will presently rise in mighty numbers; and whosoever they pretend for at first, within a while they will set up for themselves, to the utter ruin of all the nobility and gentry of the kingdom." "Rich men", a pamphleteer ironically observed later, "are none of the greatest enemies to monarchy."[1] But this fear of the common people only encouraged the king to think himself indispensable: he refused all overtures, and in the summer of 1642 war began.

In time of war men must choose one side or the other. Many gentlemen to whom property meant more than principle chose the line of least resistance and saved their estates by co-operating with whichever party dominated in

[1] *Portland Manuscripts*, Historical MSS. Commission, I p. 87; P. Chamberlen, *The Poore Mans Advocate*, 1649, p. 21.

their area. But even among the men of conviction, the dividing issues were obscured (as they have been for many historians) by the fact that many of the hated State officials were also officials of the national Church. And for the Church much traditional and sentimental popularity could be worked up. Many of the Parliamentarians, moreover, tended to speak as though they thought the most important part of their struggle the ideological battle of Puritanism against an Anglicanism that was barely distinguishable from Catholicism. But their actions make it clear that they knew that more than this was at stake.

The issue was one of political power. The bourgeoisie had rejected Charles I's Government, not because he was a bad man, but because he represented an obsolete social system. His Government tried to perpetuate a feudal social order when the conditions existed for free capitalist development, when the increase of national wealth could only come by means of free capitalist development. A seventeenth century parson thus described the line-up:—"Against the king, the laws and religion, were a company of poor tradesmen, broken and decayed citizens, deluded and priest-ridden women, . . . the rude rabble that knew not wherefore they were got together, . . . tailors, shoemakers, linkboys, etc.; . . . on the king's side . . . all the bishops of the land, all the deans, prebends and learned men; both the universities; all the princes, dukes, marquises; all the earls and lords except two or three; . . . all the knights and gentlemen in the three nations, except a score of sectaries and atheists."[1] We need not take that partisan account too literally but it makes the *class* nature of the division clear.

Charles's policy throughout his reign illustrates the class basis of his rule. He tried to regulate trade and industry, with the contradictory intention both of slowing down a too rapid capitalist development and of sharing in its profits. In foreign policy he wished for the alliance of the most reactionary powers, Spain and Austria, and refused therefore the forward national policy demanded by the bourgeoisie. Because he lost all favour with the moneyed classes, he had to levy illegal taxes, to aim to dispense with Parliament, to rule by force. His

[1] D. Lloyd, *Memoires*, 1668, p. 17.

failure in Scotland showed up the rottenness of the whole structure which he had reared; and his appeals for national unity against the foreign enemy fell on deaf ears. The real enemy was at home. The invading Scottish army was hailed as an ally. The Parliamentarian attack showed that the opposition had realised that they were fighting more than a few evil counsellors (as they had long believed or pretended to believe), more even than the King himself. They were fighting a system. Before the social order they needed could be secure they had to smash the old bureaucratic machinery, defeat the cavaliers in battle. The heads of a king and many peers had to roll in the dust before it could be certain that future kings and the peerage would recognise the dominance of the new class.

For many years during and after the Civil War, in their eagerness to defeat the old order, the moneyed classes willingly accepted taxes three and four times as heavy as those they had refused to pay to Charles I. For the objection was not to taxes as such; it was to the policy to implement which those taxes were collected. The bourgeoisie had no confidence in Charles, would not trust him with money, because they knew that the whole basis of his rule was hostility to their development. But to a government of their own kind the purse-strings were at once loosed.

Nor was it a war of the rich only. All sections of society in southern and eastern England brought in their contributions to help to win the war, for in the overthrow of the old régime men saw the essential preliminary condition of social and intellectual advance. Many of those who fought for Parliament were afterwards disappointed with the achievements of the revolution, felt they had been betrayed. But they were right to fight. A victory for Charles I and his gang could only have meant the economic stagnation of England, the stabilisation of a backward feudal society in a commercial age, and have necessitated an even bloodier struggle for liberation later. The Parliamentarians thought they were fighting God's battles. They were certainly fighting those of posterity, throwing off an intolerable incubus to further advance. The fact that the revolution might have gone further should never allow us to forget the heroism and faith and disciplined energy with which ordinary decent people responded when the Parliament's leaders freely and frankly appealed to them to support its cause.

4.

THE REVOLUTION

ONCE the war against the King had begun, divisions arose inside and outside Parliament as to the mode of conducting it. The Cavaliers, as the troops of the Royalist gentry came to be called, had certain military advantages. The Roundheads (there is a social sneer in the name) were strongest in the towns, and though the burghers brought wealth to the cause, they were not at first experienced fighting men. The Cavaliers, on the other hand, relied mainly on the north and west of England, economically backward and badly policed; they, with their tenants and dependents, were used to hard riding and fighting.

Yet for a long time Parliament tried to fight the Cavaliers with their own weapons—by calling out the feudal militia in the counties loyal to Parliament, by using the old financial and administrative machinery of the counties to run the war. But by this means the real resources of Parliament were not drawn upon—the vast wealth of London, the administrative abilities of the bourgeoisie, especially the initiative and resource of the masses of ordinary people who staunchly supported the cause, but were thwarted by the caste system of officering the militia and by its local loyalties. A royalist advance on London was only checked by the obstinate resistance of three great ports—Hull, Plymouth and Gloucester—and by the bold front presented by the citizens of London at Turnham Green (1642) and their daring march to the relief of Gloucester. But these spontaneous efforts were inadequately co-ordinated.

Oliver Cromwell first showed his genius in overcoming these weaknesses and showing that a revolutionary war must be organised in a revolutionary way. In his force in the eastern counties promotion came by merit, not birth: "I had rather have a plain russet-coated captain," he said, "that knows what he fights for and loves what he knows, than that which you call 'a gentleman' and is nothing else."[1] He insisted on his men having "the root of the matter" in them; otherwise he encouraged free discussion of divergent views. Cromwell had to fight those of his superior officers who would not adopt the democratic method of recruitment and organisation whose advantages he had shown. (This conflict is usually described in our school histories as one between " Presbyterians" and "Independents." It will be useful to retain these terms, but religion had little to do with it except in so far as Cromwell advocated freedom of assembly and discussion, i.e. "religious toleration"; the real difference was between the win-the-war party and the compromisers. It was, in fact, a class split—between the big trading bourgeoisie and that section of the aristocracy and big landowners whose interests were bound up with them—"Presbyterians"—and the progressive smaller gentry, yeomen, free-trade bourgeoisie, supported by the masses of smaller peasants and artisans—"Independents" and "Sectaries.") Many of the great "Presbyterian" commanders did not want too complete a victory. "If we beat the King ninety and nine times, yet he is King still," said the Earl of Manchester, Cromwell's general. "My Lord," Cromwell replied, "if this be so, why did we take up arms at first?"[2]

The "Presbyterians" were afraid of the flood of radical democracy to which a frank appeal to the people against the King might expose them. Cromwell himself was alleged to have said, "There would never be a good time in England till we have done with Lords." Certainly many of his troops were thinking so. The Independent and Sectarian congregations were the way in which ordinary people organised themselves in those days to escape from the propaganda of the established Church and discuss the things they wanted to discuss in their own way. The Presbyterian Edwards gave as one of the "heresies" of the Sectaries the view that "by natural birth all

[1] Carlyle, *Cromwell's Letters and Speeches*, ed. Lomas, I, p. 154.
[2] Gardiner, *History of the Great Civil War*, ed. 1893, II, p. 59.

men are equally and alike born to like property, liberty and freedom."[1] These were the small people, whose intellectual vision was not restricted by anxieties for their own property. They were invaluable for their enthusiasm, courage and morale in the army; but they came to produce what their paymasters regarded as dangerous social ideas.

Such were the difficulties the bourgeoisie experienced even at the beginning of its career; it needed the people and yet feared them, and wanted to keep the monarchy as a check against democracy—if only Charles I would act as they wanted him to, as Charles II, by and large, later did.

The "Presbyterians" hoped to rely principally upon the well-disciplined Scottish army to bear the brunt of the fighting. But after the great victory of Marston Moor, won in 1644 by Cromwell's genius and the discipline of his yeomen cavalry, he forced the issue. "It is now a time to speak or for ever to hold the tongue," he said in Parliament. The tax-paying classes were becoming irritated at the slow and dilatory tactics of the aristocratic "Presbyterian" commanders, which increased the cost of the war. A democratic reorganisation was necessary for victory over the more experienced fighters on the Royalist side.

These considerations caused Cromwell's views to prevail, and by the "Self-Denying Ordinance" all Members of Parliament were called upon to lay down their commands (April, 1645). This hit principally the peers; the abandonment of their traditional right to command the armed forces of the country was in itself a minor social revolution. The New Model Army of the career open to the talents was formed —nationally organised and financed by a new national tax.

This in its turn led to corresponding changes in the State machinery. The destruction of the royal bureaucracy had left a void which was ultimately to be filled by a new middle-class civil service. But meanwhile, pressure of revolutionary necessity had led to the creation of a series of revolutionary committees in the localities. "We had a thing here called a Committee," wrote a despondent gentleman in the Isle of Wight, "which overruled Deputy-Lieutenants and also Justices

[1] *Gangraena*, 1646, III, p. 16A.

of the Peace, and of this we had brave men: Ringwood of Newport, the pedlar: Maynard, the apothecary: Matthews, the baker: Wavell and Legge, farmers; and poor Baxter of Hurst Castle. These ruled the whole Island, and did whatsoever they thought good in their own eyes."[1] (Sir John Oglander probably exaggerated the social inferiority of his enemies: over the country as a whole the county committees were run by the gentry and the upper bourgeoisie). These committees were now organised and centralised and all brought under the unifying control of the great committees of Parliament, which really ran the Civil War—the committee of both kingdoms, the committee for advance of money, the committee for compounding, etc. The old State system was not wholly but partially destroyed and modified; new institutions were being built up under pressure of events.

In the military sense the war was won by artillery (which money alone could buy) and by Cromwell's yeomen cavalry. Under Prince Rupert, the cavaliers charged with vigour and desperation, but they were totally undisciplined, split up for plunder after the first charge. In war as in peace, the feudal gentry could never resist the prospect of loot. But Cromwell's humbler horsemen had a discipline that was irresistible because it was self-imposed. Thanks to the complete freedom of discussion which existed in the army, they "knew what they fought for and loved what they knew." So they charged home, knee to knee, reserving their fire till the last moment, then reformed and charged again and again until the enemy was broken. The Parliament's battles were won because of the discipline and unity and high political consciousness of the masses organised in the New Model Army.

Once properly organised and regularly paid, with an efficient commissariat and technical staff, with Cromwell, the indispensable leader, reappointed to his command, the New Model Army advanced rapidly to victory and the Royalists were decisively routed at Naseby (1645). After that the war soon ended. A Royalist commander, surrendering, said: "You have done your work and may go play—unless you fall out among yourselves."

[1] Bamford, *A Royalist's Notebook*, p. 110.

That was the danger. For once the fighting was over, the "Presbyterian" compromisers began to raise their heads again, inside and outside Parliament. Charles had surrendered to the Scottish army in 1646, who sold him to the English Parliament. Thereupon the "Presbyterians" began to negotiate with the captive King: they proposed to get rid of the victorious Army by sending it to conquer Ireland, without paying its wages; they produced no social reforms, not even an indemnity for actions committed during the war, so that soldiers were actually brought before the courts for what they had done in the service of Parliament.

But as the opponents of the New Model Army had anticipated, the people were not so easily to be fobbed off, once they were armed and given the chance of organisation. The main obstacle to a peasant and artisan population making its will felt is the difficulty of organising the petty bourgeoisie; but the radicals saw the Army as an organisation which could " teach peasants to understand liberty."[1] In London a political party sprang up to represent the views of the small producers, which got into touch with the Army agitation. These were the Levellers.

The trouble came to a head in the Army in the spring of 1647 with the attempt to disband regiments and form new ones for the Irish service. Led by the yeomen cavalry, the rank and file organised themselves, appointed deputies from each regiment ("agitators," they were called) to a central council, pledged themselves to maintain solidarity and not disband until their demands were satisfied. There was a high degree of organisation—a party chest and levy on members, a printing press, contacts with London, with the other armies and garrisons, and with the fleet. The initiative in this mass movement seems undoubtedly to have come from the rank and file, though many of the lower officers co-operated enthusiastically from the start. The general officers ("grandees" as the Levellers called them) hesitated for a time, tried to mediate between the "Presbyterian" majority in Parliament and the Army rank and file. Then, when they saw the latter were determined to

[1] The Rev. Hugh Peter, *Mr. Peters Last Report of the English Wars*, 1646, p. 6.

proceed, they threw themselves in with the movement and henceforth concentrated on guiding its energies into their own channels. They worked principally to restrict the soldiers' demands to the professional and political, and to minimise the social and economic programme which the Levellers tried to graft on to the rank-and-file movement.

Army and Parliament now existed side by side as rival powers in the State. In June, 1647, in order to stop the "Presbyterians" in Parliament coming to an agreement with the King behind the backs of the Army, Cornet Joyce was sent by the agitators (though probably with Cromwell's connivance) to seize Charles. At a general rendezvous next day, the whole Army took a solemn "Engagement" not to divide until the liberties of England were secure. An Army Council was set up in which elected representatives of the rank and file sat side by side with officers to decide questions of policy. England has never again seen such democratic control of the Army as existed for the next six months. Then, holding the King as a bargaining weapon, the Army marched on London. The principal "Presbyterian" leaders withdrew from the House of Commons, leaving Cromwell and the "Independents" temporarily in control; the Army was in a position decisively to influence policy.

That was as much as the gentlemen "Independents" wanted. They had removed their main rivals and were perfectly satisfied with the old system (with or without the King). They had no desire to modify it further, so long as they had the running of it. But the petty bourgeoisie, whose interests were more and more being expressed by the Levellers, wanted vast changes. And Leveller influence was growing rapidly in the Army. They wanted complete free trade for small producers, as well as the freedom of the big merchant companies from the corrupt monopolies which Parliament had already abolished; they wanted disestablishment of the Church and the abolition of tithes; security of small property and reform of the debtors' law; and to secure all this they wanted a republic, extension of the parliamentary franchise, manhood suffrage.

These were the points at issue in debates of the Army Council held at Putney in October and November, 1647, on the proposed Leveller constitution, the Agreement of the People. The Leveller Rainborowe wanted manhood suffrage, because he thought "the poorest he that is in England hath a life to live as the greatest he."[1] Ireton, Cromwell's son-in-law, summed up the Grandees' case when he said: "Liberty cannot be provided for in a general sense, if property be preserved."[2] An attempt by the Levellers to capture control of the Army was defeated by the Grandees at Ware in November, 1647, and resulted in the dispersal of the Army Council and the end of Army democracy. But meanwhile the King had escaped from captivity, civil war broke out again in the following May, and this reunited the Army behind Cromwell.

After the Army's victory in this second civil war, Grandees and Levellers united to clear the compromisers out of Parliament (Pride's Purge) and to bring the King to justice. After a speedy trial, he was executed on January 30th, 1649, as a "public enemy to the good people of this nation." Monarchy was declared to be "unnecessary, burdensome, and dangerous to the libery, safety and public interest of the people," and was abolished. The House of Lords, which was also abolished, was merely "useless and dangerous." On May 19th, 1649, a republic was proclaimed. But the Agreement of the People, the extension of the franchise, the economic and social demands of the Levellers, were as far from attainment as ever; they felt they had been betrayed. The Grandees were able to provoke them into an unsuccessful revolt, which was isolated and put down and its leaders shot at Burford in May, 1649.

It is not difficult to account for the failure of the Levellers. Their demands were those of the petty bourgeoisie, a class always unstable and difficult to organise because of its dependence, economic and ideological, on the big bourgeoisie (cf. the impotence of present-day liberal morality to control a rapidly changing world). Moreover, the petty bourgeoisie in the seventeenth century was in the process of stratification. For if some of the richer yeomen and artisans were prospering and pushing their way up into the bourgeoisie and gentry, many more were being squeezed down to the status of landless

[1] Woodhouse, *Puritanism and Liberty*, p. 53. Rainborowe was subsequently assassinated by Royalist desperadoes. [2] *Ibid.*, p. 73.

agricultural labourers. The events of the Civil War speeded up this process. Many of the most successful and influential members of the petty bourgeoisie found they had interests in common with those of the bourgeoisie, like the *kulaks* in the Rusian Revolution. Both, for instance, welcomed enclosure and the employment of wage labour in production for the market. Consequently this section deserted the Leveller movement as soon as it ceased to be merely the most revolutionary wing of the bourgeoisie and began itself to attack the big bourgeoisie. The section which was sinking in the social scale tended to be erratic, despairing and defeatist. The Leveller ideal was a small-producer's Utopia in economics and petty-bourgeois democracy in politics. Despite the focus of the Army, the Levellers never represented a sufficiently homogeneous class to be able to achieve their aims. The full realisation of the democratic tasks even of the bourgeois revolution is impossible unless there is a working class able to carry them out. The most radical achievements of the English bourgeois revolution (abolition of the monarchy, confiscation of Church, Crown and aristocratic estates) were put through by what Engels called the "plebeian methods" of the Levellers and "Independents"; but there was no organised working-class movement, with a vision of a different form of social order and a scientific revolutionary theory, to lead the petty bourgeoisie to a frontal attack on the power of big capital. After the Burford shootings, the Leveller movement degenerated. Many of its leaders turned careerist or speculated in land; other took to terrorism, sometimes even in agreement with the Royalists. Many more had their energies diverted by the radical religious movements which date from this period—notably the pacifist Quakers, the anarchist Anabaptists and Fifth Monarchists.

The nearest the English bourgeois revolution got to representing the interests of the propertiless was the Digger movement. This was an attempt to proceed by direct action to a form of agrarian communism by members of the dispossessed rural proletariat, who argued that lords of manors had been defeated as well as the King, that the victory of the people had freed the land of England, which was now theirs to cultivate.

Transferring Rainborowe's slogan from politics to economics, the Digger Gerrard Winstanley wrote: "The poorest man hath as true a title and just right to the land as the richest man."[1] In the spring of 1649 a group of Diggers began to dig up the waste land on St. George's Hill in Surrey. Indignant local gentlemen and parsons called in the soldiery, and the communistic colony was ultimately dispersed. There were similar attempts in Kent, Buckinghamshire and Northamptonshire, but the movement reached no great dimensions, representing as it did a small if growing class; its weakness is evidenced in the pacifism and passive resistance its leaders preached.

Winstanley's communist ideal was in one sense backward-looking, since it arose from the village community which capitalism was already disintegrating. But the Diggers were the most radical and most egalitarian opponents of the feudal social order. Winstanley's clear and simple statements have a contemporary ring: "This is the bondage the poor complain of, that they are kept poor by their brethren in a land where there is so much plenty for everyone."[2] "Every one talks of freedom, but there are but few that act for freedom, and the actors for freedom are oppressed by the talkers and verbal professors of freedom." For "it is clearly seen that if we be suffered to speak, we shall batter to pieces all the old laws, and prove the maintainers of them hypocrites and traitors to the commonwealth of England."[3] And Winstanley did not only look to the past; he also had glimpses of a future in which "wheresoever there is a people united by common community of livelihood into oneness it will be the strongest land in the world, for there they will be as one man to defend their inheritance."[4]

* * * * *

The history of the English Revolution from 1649 to 1660 can be briefly told. Cromwell's shooting of the Levellers at Burford made a restoration of monarchy and lords ultimately inevitable, for the breach of big bourgeoisie and gentry with

[1] Ed. Hamilton, *Selections from the Works of Gerrard Winstanley*, p. 69.
[2] *Ibid.*, p. 157. [3] *Ibid.*, pp. 68, 74. [4] *Ibid.*, p. 42.

the popular forces meant that their government could only be maintained either by an army (which in the long run proved crushingly expensive as well as difficult to control) or by a compromise with the surviving representatives of the old order. But first there were still tasks to be done.

(1) There was the conquest of Ireland, the expropriation of its landowners and peasantry—the first big triumph of English imperialism and the first big defeat of English democracy. For the petty bourgeoisie of the Army, despite the warnings of many of the Leveller leaders, allowed themselves to be distracted from establishing their own liberties in England and, deluded by religious slogans, to destroy those of the Irish. Many of them set up as landed proprietors in Ireland. (The Leveller revolt of 1649 had been occasioned by the refusal of many of the rank and file to leave for Ireland, for that meant violating their Engagement of 1647 not to divide until the liberties of England were secure.)

(2) There was the conquest of Scotland, necessary to prevent a restoration of the old order thence; Scotland was opened up to English traders by political union.

(3) A forward commercial policy was undertaken with the Navigation Act of 1651, the basis of England's commercial prosperity in the next century. This aimed at winning the carrying trade of Europe for English ships, and at excluding all rivals from trade with England's colonies. It led to a war with the Dutch, who had monopolised the carrying trade of the world in the first half of the seventeenth century. For in that period the royal policy had frustrated all attempts of the bourgeoisie to throw the resources of England into an effective struggle for this trade. In this war, thanks to Blake's fleet and the economic strength the Republican Government was able to mobilise, England was victorious.

(4) An imperialist policy needed the strong Navy which Charles had failed to build up, and under Blake the Commonwealth began to rule the waves to some purpose; war in alliance with France against Spain brought Jamaica and Dunkirk to England.

(5) The abolition of feudal tenures meant that landlords

established an absolute right to *their* property vis-à-vis the King; the failure of copyholders to win equal security for *their* holdings left them at the mercy of their landlords, and prepared the way for the wholesale enclosures and expropriations of the next 150 years.

(6) A violent restoration of the old order at home was made impossible by demolishing fortresses, disarming the Cavaliers, and taxing them to the verge of ruin, so that many were forced to sell their estates and with them their claim to social prestige and political power. For many owners of economically undeveloped estates who were already desperately in debt, the period of the Commonwealth and after represented a great foreclosing on mortgages, capital at last getting its own back against improvident landlords.

(7) Finally, to finance the new activities of the revolutionary governments, the lands of Church and Crown and of many leading Royalists were confiscated and sold; smaller Royalists whose estates had been confiscated were allowed to "compound" for them by paying a fine equal to a substantial proportion of their estates (and they were thus often compelled to sell a part of their property privately to be able to keep the remainder).

If we keep these points in mind, there is no need to go into the detailed political revolutions of the next eleven years. Cromwell dissolved the Long Parliament forcibly in 1653, nominated a convention of his own adherents (the Barebones Parliament), which revived the social and economic demands of the petty bourgeoisie and had to be hastily dissolved. Cromwell was then proclaimed Protector under a Constitution (the "Instrument of Government"), which was rigged to conceal the dictatorship of the Army officers. He called a Parliament under this constitution on a new £200 franchise, by which moneyed men were admitted to vote and the lesser freeholders excluded. But Parliament and Army quarrelled, Parliament was dissolved, and a period of naked military dictatorship followed under the Major-Generals, in which the Cavaliers were finally disarmed. Ultimately Cromwell and his Court circle (representing especially the new civil service), under pressure from the City, came to realise that the Army had done its job and that its maintenance now meant a crushing burden of taxation on the propertied classes, for which no compensating advantages were obtained.

Moreover, despite repeated purges and the drafting of politically unreliable units to fight in Ireland, Jamaica, Flanders, the Leveller and democratic tradition remained strong in the Army. So in 1657 Cromwell surrendered to his second Parliament and accepted a new parliamentary constitution. This constitution (the "Humble Petition and Advice") took executive power from a council representing the Army Grandees and placed it in one controlled by Parliament, brought the Army under Parliament's financial control, made the protectorate non-elective and the Protector subject to Parliamentary control. The new constitution was introduced by a City Member, and was supported by many former Presbyterians who were soon to welcome home Charles II. Protests in the Army only just prevented Oliver accepting the Crown as King. The Grandees were bought off by being given seats in a new second chamber.

But Cromwell died in 1658 before this constitution was working satisfactorily; his son and successor, Richard Cromwell, lacked his influence with the Army; and the Petition and Advice constitution was so like a monarchy that it was clear that the bourgeoisie would accept Charles II if he would accept them, and if the Army could be disposed of. When the Grandees deposed Richard Cromwell in a palace revolution and seized power for themselves, a revulsion occurred. The English army of occupation in Scotland, under command of the ex-Royalist adventurer General Monck, had hitherto taken no part in English political intrigues. Monck had concentrated on purging it of left-wing elements and enforcing "discipline." Now he became the hope of the conservative classes in the State, frightened of the radicalism of the English armies. Monck took charge of the situation. With the approval and financial backing of the Scottish gentry, he marched down from Scotland with his purged and disciplined army, and declared for a free Parliament elected on the old franchise, to the applause of the bourgeoisie and gentry. For all knew that a "free" Parliament meant the dominance of the landed classes. "Freedom" is a relative term. This Parliament recalled Charles II in May, 1660.

That is very briefly what happened. Now let us try to see why it happened. The most conspicuous feature of the 'fifties is the growing conservatism of the "Independent" leaders; their increasing fear of social revolution as they themselves became sated and reassimilated to the "Presbyterians." This is especially evident in the class split within the Army (so powerful through its unity in 1647 and in December, 1648-January, 1649.) After the breach with the Levellers, the scramble for confiscated lands had helped to widen this split, for officers had bought lands with debentures (promises to pay wages) purchased at a discount from their troops. The rank and file, after receiving a piece of paper in lieu of wages for risking their lives in the Parliament's cause, were lucky if they got 7*s.* 6*d.* in the £1 for those pieces of paper. Many got far less—1*s.* 6*d.* or 2*s.* But for those who were rich enough to be able to wait, the "debentures" were a profitable investment. After 1657 the lower officers also felt themselves betrayed by the Grandees, who had sold out for seats in the new Upper House. Fear of the possibility of a political reunion between lower officers and Army rank and file helps to account for the haste with which Charles II was scrambled home.

For by 1654 the land transfers had been completed; a new class of landowners had appeared, who now wanted peace and order to develop their property. The "Independent" gentry—Oliver Cromwell's class—had been the spearhead of the revolution because they wanted to abolish the monopoly of social and political privileges attached to *feudal* landholding and to extend them to the advantage of their own class. They had no desire to abolish big property in land as such, and the left-wing parties advocating this ceased to be useful allies and became dangerous foes as the "Independent" gentry succeeded to the position of the old ruling class. The attack on tithes made the owners of impropriations[1] see unsuspected virtues even in the old Church establishment, whilst the "excesses" of the democratic sects—Quakers and the like—

[1] *See* p. 33.

made the squirearchy yearn for an established State Church, uniform and disciplined and undemocratic.

In industry the interregnum saw attempts to organise small producers ("the yeomanry") against the power of merchant capital. In a bitter class struggle, wages were forced up. Add to this the financial difficulties, the arbitrary taxation which the Government was forced to impose after the exhaustion of the land fund (for Parliament refused to vote taxes for the Army) and we can understand the willingness of the new ruling class to compromise with the old, to agree to a restoration of the old law to guarantee the new order.

The Restoration, then, was by no means a restoration of the old régime. It is evidence, not of the weakness of the bourgeoisie and gentry, but of their strength. The personnel of the Civil Service, judicial bench, Government financiers, continued with very little change after 1660. Charles II came back, and pretended he had been King by divine hereditary right ever since his father's head had fallen on the scaffold at Whitehall. But he was not restored to his father's old position. The prerogative courts were not restored, and so Charles had no independent executive authority.[1] The common law, as adapted by Sir Edward Coke to the needs of capitalist society, triumphed alike over the arbitrary interference of the Crown and the reforming demands of the Levellers. There was no rationalisation of the legal system in the English Revolution comparable to the *Code Napoléon* which the French Revolution produced for the protection of small property. After 1701 subordination of judges to Parliament was a point of the Constitution: the gentry dominated local government as Justices of the Peace. The King had no power of taxation independent of Parliament (though by a lack of foresight Parliament in its enthusiasm voted Charles the Customs revenue for life, and such was the expansion of trade in his reign that towards the end of it he came near to financial independence. This was rectified after 1688). Charles was called King by the Grace of God, but was really King by the grace of the merchants

[1] The executive was controlled first by the impeachment of Ministers when Parliament disapproved of their conduct, then by the development of the cabinet system.

and squires. He himself recognised this when he said he didn't want to go on his travels again. James II was less wise in recognising the limitations of his position—and he travelled.

The bishops also came home with the King, but the Church did not regain its old independent power, nor its monopoly in the manufacture of public opinion. The Court of High Commission was not restored; the lesser ecclesiastical courts gradually ceased to be able to get their sentences enforced; Convocation abandoned its claim to tax the clergy independently of Parliament. The Church of England ceased even to pretend to be all-embracing and aimed at holding Nonconformists in subjection rather than at reabsorbing them. It ceased to be an instrument of power, and became the hallmark of respectability. The recognised existence of Nonconformity dates from the Restoration: State and Church were no longer identical. A separate lower middle-class culture grew up. No longer a powerful organ of government at the disposal of the King, the Church of England sank to be merely the richest of many rival religious organisations. And it too became dependent on Parliament. The bishops had been Charles I's most faithful tools; it was the bishops who first refused obedience to James II.

Some of the rich Royalists had bought their lands back before 1660. Others got them back then. Church and Crown lands were restored, too. But the mass of smaller Royalists, who had sold their estates privately after ruining themselves in the cause, got no redress. And even where landowners were restored, they were not restored on the old conditions. Feudal tenures had been abolished in 1646, and confirmation of their abolition was the first business Parliament turned its attention to after recalling the King in 1660; the absolute property rights of big landlords were secure. Between 1646 and 1660 many of the confiscated lands had passed into the possession of speculative purchasers, mostly bourgeois, who had improved cultivation, enclosed, racked rents up to the market level. The returned Royalists had perforce to adapt themselves to the new free market conditions, i.e. to turn themselves into *capitalist* farmers or lessors of their estates, or they went under in the competitive struggle.

Many of the landowners restored in 1660 had mortgaged and resold their estates by the end of the century. Among these landowners we must include the King, who henceforth became dependent on a Parliamentary civil list, a salaried official, the first Civil Servant. The King could no longer "live of his own" on his private income from his estates and feudal dues, and so could never be independent again. In the eighteenth century he had influence but no independent power. On the other hand, the failure of the democratic movement to win legally watertight security of tenure for small peasant proprietors had left the door open for ruthless racking of rents, enclosures, evictions, the creation of a landless proletariat, with no redress from a Parliament and a judicial system dominated by the propertiedc, classes.

In the business world, monopolies and royal control of industry and trade disappear for ever. Gilds and apprentice laws had broken down in the interregnum, and no effective attempt was made to revive them. Liberated trade and industry expanded rapidly. There was no break in commercial, imperial or foreign policy at the Restoration. The Navigation Act was renewed by Charles II's Government and became the backbone of English policy, the means by which the English merchants monopolised the wealth of the colonies. The exclusive trading companies declined, except where special circumstances made their retention necessary to the bourgeoisie (the East India Company). The complete domination of the moneyed interests was not established till after the second revolution in 1688, with the foundation of the Bank of England and the National Debt (1694). The years from 1660 to 1688 are a period of retrenchment, in which wealth was accumulated to finance grandiose imperialist policies which the Protectorate had undertaken and been unable to carry through. By the end of the century they were being resumed, now under the complete control of a Parliament representing landed and moneyed interests fundamentally united by their similar ways of producing wealth.

Technology likewise benefitted enormously by the liberation of science and by the stimulus to free thought and experiment which the Revolution gave. The revolutions in industrial and agrarian technique which were to change the face of England in the eighteenth century would have been impossible without the political revolution of the seventeenth century. The freedom of intellectual speculation in late seventeenth- and eighteenth-century England enormously influenced the ideas of the French Revolution of 1789.

In 1660 passive obedience was preached in all pulpits; a King was brought back "with plenty of holy oil about him," because this was necessary for Parliament, for the possessing classes, threatened by social revolution from below. A white terror was introduced by the returned *émigrés*, and an attempt was made to drive from political life all who did not accept the restored régime in Church and State (the Clarendon Code, the Test Act). Educational advances, like the purge which had made Oxford a centre of scientific research, were reversed. All this broke the revolutionary-democratic movement for the moment, though it fought back again in the sixteen-seventies and-eighties. In 1662 a Presbyterian minister, who had been deprived of his living by the Restoration, wrote in words that recapture the fears of many respectable members of the possessing classes at that time:

> "Though soon after the settlement of the nation we saw ourselves the despised and cheated party . . . yet in all this I have suffered since, I look upon it as less than my trouble was from my fears then . . . Then we lay at the mercy and impulse of a giddy, hot-headed, bloody multitude."[1]

Many Presbyterians conformed to the Church of England, now again fashionable. But the very parsons and gentry who preached passive obedience to constituted authority in 1660 united to expel James II in 1688, when he made the mistake of taking these theories at their face value and threatened to restore the old absolutist monarchy. James was hustled out by the "Glorious Revolution" of 1688, "glorious" because bloodless and because there was no social disorder, no "anarchy," no possibility of a revival of revolutionary-democratic demands.

[1] H. Newcome, *Autobiography*, I. pp. 118-19 (Chetham Soc., Vol. 26).

Ever since then orthodox historians have done their utmost to stress the "continuity" of English history, to minimise the revolutionary breaks, to pretend that the "interregnum" (the word itself shows what they are trying to do) was an unfortunate accident, that in 1660 we returned to the old Constitution normally developing, that 1688 merely corrected the aberrations of a deranged King. Whereas, in fact, the period 1640-60 saw the destruction of one kind of state and the introduction of a new political structure within which capitalism could freely develop. For tactical reasons, the ruling class in 1660 *pretended* that they were merely restoring the old forms of the Constitution. But they intended by that restoration to give sanctity and social stamp to a new social order. The important thing is that the social order was new and would not have been won without revolution.

> "If writings be true," said the Leveller Rainborowe in 1647, "there have been many scufflings between the honest men of England and those that have tyrannised over them; and if it be read, there is none of those just and equitable laws that the people of England are born to but are intrenchment altogether. But . . . if the people find that they are not suitable to freemen as they are, I know no reason should deter me . . . from endeavouring by all means to gain anything that might be of more advantage to them than the government under which they live."[1]

It is struggle that wins reforms, just as it is struggle that will retain the liberties which our ancestors won for us. And if the people find the legal system "not suitable to freedom as it is," then it can be changed by united action. That is the lesson of the seventeenth century for to-day. It was of us that Winstanley was thinking when he wrote at the head of one of his most impassioned pamphlets:

> "*When these clay bodies are in grave, and children stand in place,*
> *This shews we stood for truth and peace and freedom in our days.*"[2]

[1] Woodhouse, *Puritan and Liberty*, p. 14.
[2] Winstanley, *Selections*, p. 66.

"Freedom," he added with a bitterness born of experience, but also with pride and confidence, "freedom is the man that will turn the world upside down, therefore no wonder he hath enemies." And freedom for Winstanley was not a cheap politician's slogan: it meant the living struggle of comrades to build a society based on communal ownership, a society which ordinary people would think worth defending with all their might because it was *their* society. "True freedom lies in the community in spirit and community in the earthly treasury."[1]

> "This commonwealth's freedom will unite the hearts of Englishmen together in love, so that if a foreign enemy endeavour to come in, we shall all with joint consent rise up to defend our inheritance, and shall be true to one another. Whereas now the poor see, if they fight and should conquer the enemy, yet either they or their children are like to be slaves still, for the gentry will have all."[2]
>
> "Property . . . divides the whole world into parties, and is the cause of all wars and bloodshed and contention everywhere."
>
> "When the earth becomes a common treasury again, as it must, . . . then this enmity in all lands will cease."[3]

We still have much to learn from the seventeenth century.

[1] Winstanley, *Selections*, pp. 67-8.
[2] *Ibid.*, p. 103.
[3] *Ibid.*, pp. 42, 38.

SOME BOOKS FOR FURTHER READING

Those marked with an asterisk are by Marxists

1. GENERAL.

*A. L. Morton, *A People's History of England*, in conjunction with *Daphne May's *Study Guide to the People's History of England.*

*M. H. Dobb, *Studies in the Development of Capitalism.*

*C. Hill, " The English Civil War in the Writings of Marx and Engels ", *Science and Society*, 1948.

2. ECONOMIC BACKGROUND.

*K. Marx, *Capital*, Vol. I, ed. Dona Torr, chapters XXVI-VIII.

*V. I. Lenin, *Development of Capitalism in Russia* (Selected Works, Vol. I). Describes a state of society very similar to seventeenth century England.

*Ed. M. H. Dobb, *The Transition from Feudalism to Capitalism.*

*K. Kautsky, *Thomas More and his Utopia.*

R. H. Tawney, *The Agrarian Problem in the Sixteenth Century.*

G. N. Clark, *The Wealth of England, 1496-1760.*

J. U. Nef, *Industry and Government in France and England, 1540-1640*

J. U. Nef, " The Progress of Technology and the Growth of Large Scale Industry in Great Britain, 1540-1640 ", *Economic History Review*, 1934.

R. H. Tawney, " The Rise of the Gentry, 1558-1640 ", *Economic History Review*, 1941.

L. Stone, " An Anatomy of the Elizabethan Aristocracy ", *Economic History Review*, 1948, followed by a number of articles by H. R. Trevor-Roper and R. H. Tawney in succeeding issues of the journal.

E. Kerridge, " The Movement of Rent, 1540-1640 ", *Economic History Review*, 1953.

3. RELIGION.

R. H. Tawney, *Religion and the Rise of Capitalism.*

H. C. White, *Social Criticism in Popular Religious Literature of the Sixteenth Century.*

W. Haller, *The Rise of Puritanism.*

R. B. Schlatter, *Social Ideas of Religious Leaders, 1660-88.*

M. James, " The Political Importance of the Tithes Controversy in the English Revolution ", *History*, 1941.

*S. F. Mason, " Science and Religion in Seventeenth Century England," *Past and Present*, 1953.

4. THE REVOLUTION.

E. Bernstein, *Cromwell and Communism.*

C. H. Firth, *Cromwell's Army.*

M. James, *Social Policy during the Puritan Revolution.*

H. Holorenshaw, *The Levellers and the English Revolution.*

Ed. C. Hill and E. Dell, *The Good Old Cause.*

*J. Lindsay, *Civil War in England.*

**The Modern Quarterly*, Spring 1949. Tercentenary number, 1649-1949.

*C. Hill, "Soviet Interpretations of the Interregnum", *Economic History Review*, 1938.

*C. Hill, "The Agrarian Legislation of the Interregnum", *English Historical Review*, 1940.

*C. Hill, "The English Revolution and the Brotherhood of Man", *Science and Society*, 1954.

*E. Hobsbawm, "The Crisis of the Seventeenth Century," *Past and Present*, Nos. 5 and 6, 1954

5. POLITICAL IDEAS.

Ed. A. S. P. Woodhouse, *Puritanism and Liberty.* Contains the debates in the Army Council in 1647.

Ed. D. M. Wolfe, *Leveller Manifestoes.* A collection of documents.

Ed. W. Haller and G. Davies, *Leveller Tracts, 1647-53.* Documents.

Ed. L. D. Hamilton, *Selections from the Works of Gerrard Winstanley.*

D. W. Petegorsky, *Left-Wing Democracy in the English Civil War.* A study of Winstanley.

D. M. Wolfe, *Milton in the Puritan Revolution.*

H. J. Laski, *The Rise of European Liberalism.*

P. Zagorin, *A History of Political Thought in the English Revolution.*

*A. L. Morton, *The English Utopia.*

*C. Hill, "The Norman Yoke", in *Democracy and the Labour Movement*, ed. J. Saville.

6. AFTER 1660.

*Iris Morley, *A Thousand Lives.* Monmouth's Rebellion of 1685.

*C. E. Gore, "The 250th Anniversary of the 'Glorious' Revolution of 1688", *Communist International*, 1938.

*B. Hessen, "Social and Economic Roots of Newton's *Principia*", in *Science at the Cross Roads*, 1931.

7. NOVELS.

*J. Lindsay, *1649.*

*M. Slater, *Englishmen with Swords.*

8. IN RUSSIAN.

Ed. E. A. Kosminsky and Y. A. Levitsky, *The English Bourgeois Revolution of the 17th century*, 2 vols., Moscow, 1954. The most comprehensive work in any language.